LET'S CAMP!

Shelley Rotner

Millbrook Press / Minneapolis

Are you ready for an adventure in nature?

Let's go camping!

First, we'll need to get ready.

Let's make a list!

We need lots of gear.

And food!

Let's **PACK** the car.
Then, off we go to
the campground!

We're here!

This is our campsite,

where we'll stay overnight.

We **PITCH** our tent

and settle in.

DARLING TRAIL
DAR FIRE TOWER 0.6
LOOP W/ LONG TRAIL
LOOP W/ NEMBA

Time to **EXPLORE**!

Let's **HIKE**, **RIDE**,

and **BIKE** . . .

PADDLE, **FISH**, and **SWIM**.

We **FIND** animals that hop, slither, and crawl.

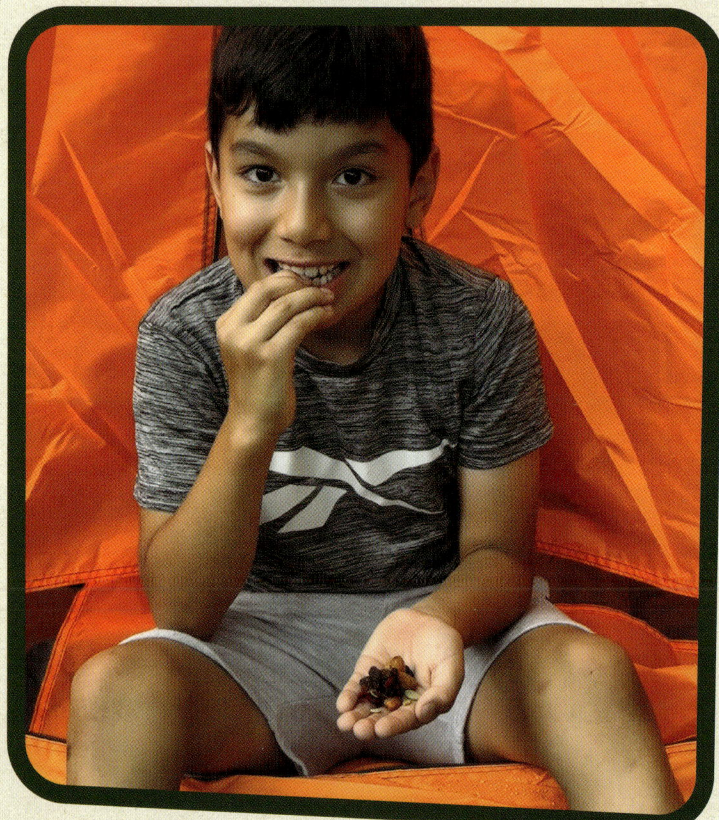

We **RELAX**, **SNACK**, and **PLAY** games at our campsite.

When we get hungry, we have yummy food to **COOK** and **EAT**!

Nighttime is coming.

There's the moon!

Time to **BUILD** a fire,

SHARE stories, and

ROAST marshmallows

for s'mores.

Let's get ready for bed. We'll be cozy and comfortable in our tent!

I think I **HEAR** an owl hooting.

It's time to **SLEEP** and **DREAM** of our next adventure.

NATURE SPY GUIDE

It's morning!

Time to **EAT** breakfast and **PACK** up.

Our fun camping trip has come to an end.

We hope we do this again soon!

S'more Recipe

Ingredients: marshmallows, graham crackers, chocolate bars

You'll need: skewers or sticks

1. Put your marshmallows on a skewer or stick. Break up chocolate bars and graham crackers. Place chocolate on one half of the graham cracker.
2. Roast your marshmallows over the fire to your liking.
3. Place the roasted marshmallows on top of the chocolate on one graham cracker. Then use a second cracker to hold the marshmallows in place while you remove the skewer or stick.
4. Enjoy!

Planning and Packing

- Check the weather forecast before your trip. That way you can prepare for all kinds of weather.
- Pack clothing you can layer if the weather gets warmer or cooler.
- Hats can keep you warm—or protect you from the sun. You'll also need the right shoes and boots for hiking and other activities.

Safety

- Store food and garbage in a cooler, a bear-proof container, or your car to keep it safely away from animals such as bears, racoons, squirrels, and chipmunks.
- No running around campfires!
- Always wait for a grown-up to help with campfires and fire safety. Make sure to fully put out campfires before leaving the campsite.

Campground Guidelines

- Try not to make noise that could disturb your neighboring campsites.
- Avoid going into other campsites unless the campers invite you.
- Always pick up trash at your campsite and on trails.
- Stay on the paths.
- If you plan to fish, check the rules for the area.

Campground Activities

- Some campgrounds have park rangers that offer programs and who can answer questions. Some also have nature shacks that have exhibits, collections, and taxidermy specimens of local animals.
- Geocaching is an activity that uses GPS (Global Positioning System) and navigational techniques to hide and seek containers.
- You can bring containers to use for making small terrariums or temporary homes for insects or animals such as frogs and salamanders. Be sure to gently release your nature guest back where you found it.
- Some campgrounds have playgrounds or sports areas for group games such as baseball, soccer, Frisbee, or football.

To all the campers, nature lovers, and our future stewards.

Millbrook Press™
An imprint of Lerner Publishing Group, Inc.
241 First Avenue North
Minneapolis, MN 55401 USA

For reading levels and more information, look up this title at www.lernerbooks.com.

Background: Kiwihug/Unsplash.

Designed by Athena Currier.
Main body text set in Mikado. Typeface provided by HVD Fonts.

Library of Congress Cataloging-in-Publication Data

Names: Rotner, Shelley author
Title: Let's camp! / Shelley Rotner.
Other titles: Let us camp!
Description: Minneapolis : Millbrook Press, [2026] | Audience: Ages 4–9 | Audience: Grades K–1 | Summary: "Experience a camping trip from beginning to end. Colorful photos and simple text show everything from planning and packing to setting up camp and sleeping in a tent, with lots of fun along the way!" —Provided by publisher.
Identifiers: LCCN 2025022313 (print) | LCCN 2025022314 (ebook) | ISBN 9798765670477 lib. bdg. | ISBN 9798765670484 pbk. | ISBN 9798765699867 epub
Subjects: LCSH: Camping—Juvenile literature | Outdoor recreation for children
Classification: LCC GV192.2 .R68 2026 (print) | LCC GV192.2 (ebook) | DDC 796.54—dc23/eng/20250621

LC record available at https://lccn.loc.gov/2025022313
LC ebook record available at https://lccn.loc.gov/2025022314

Manufactured in the United States of America
1-1012839-54072-8/13/2025